May these words rest tenderly within your heart.

All my love (and then some),
Bethany Cole

I have made beautiful memories with lovers who now live as echoes in my mind.

But I would never take those memories away for the sake of not going through the heartbreak of losing them.

That is what love is to me.

Maybe even life.

Isn't all life uncertain?

Because when do we ever know anything with absolute certainty? And even if we know, how often do those things fluctuate like the ocean tide?

Does love not deserve to exist in these spaces of uncertainty?

I've started seeing life as love despite not knowing what will be next; the canvas is a blank slate before me.

Uncertainty has no consolation for the timing of our heart's desires. So, I'm learning to let love exist in these unknown waters.

Uncertainty will come and go like the rising tide.

But like the ocean herself, love remains.

Holding yourself tight but knowing it's okay to wish you could pass the baton to someone else occasionally.

Because this is a *human* feeling.

This feeling of a connection that admires your fragments and still sees you as whole.

A feeling which speaks, "Rest your weary bones against my shoulder tonight."

I wanted to find my balance.

To allow myself to rest and not see it as inadequate. To push myself into discomfort and still feel safe. Let myself desire to be held, but know I can save myself.

To go with the flow but still have intention. To stand in the pouring rain and still feel the sun's warmth.

To leave this earth a little more kind and to know it's okay not to fix it completely.

To know it *still matters, still counts.*

The space where grace lives, breaths are deep, and fragility is *embraced.*

Reminding myself this ebb and flow is always present and always beautiful.

Like the ocean waves going back and forth against the shore.

I didn't want to speak too soon, but I often feared not speaking soon enough, for I thought ceaselessly of the fragility of life.

I wasn't sure when so many rules were added to the game of love or when it started becoming a game.

For I only knew it as something that was.

We become accustomed to our surroundings.

They say even the most beautiful ocean views become less and less admired over time.

It's no wonder we fear love.

How are we to compete with the *entire* ocean?

The terrifying part of love is the inevitable endings: the love you had and then lost or the love you almost had.

Can we look at such anguish and mend it into joy?

For the love we had and the undeniable love that remains.

Even after all the endings, our souls stretched beyond the vessels in our weary hearts.

Proclaiming, *"I can still love here."*

To be or not to be

I say to myself as I pluck sunflower petals. Each one falling onto the sidewalk.

I never finish, afraid it will leave me with those three words: not to be.

I want to ask you myself, but what if it's too early? What if you haven't even thought about it at all?

I want to ask the universe if it can tell me how this will turn out.

If it can let me know beforehand so I can soften the blow to my heart even a little bit.

I know it doesn't work this way, and I shouldn't assume love is some ticking time bomb. You are leaving me feeling that, at any given moment, it could implode into a million pieces.

No matter how terrifying it feels, I don't want to shield my heart from the endless amounts of 'what ifs.' Because I'm learning, I deserve to feel the sun's warmth as much as the sunflowers.

Regardless of whether they are
to be or not to be.

The truth is…

I'm terrified love will leave me standing in the pouring rain with no raincoat—my bare feet against the damp cement.

I don't mind the rain or standing barefoot in its puddles.

It's the standing alone part, leaving an ache for the love you thought would stay despite the rain.

But some people are not meant to stay
and it has very little to do with you or the love you
give.

So maybe
all these puddles
of temporary lovers are leading us
to the ocean of love we deserve.

I know this magical place we can escape to. It's open year-round, and sometimes parking is an absolute nightmare. But this spot is unfound, and my God, isn't that quite rare?

To find a place untouched by all this commotion.

Sometimes, I run there as the sun prepares to say good night. It's the only thing that has seemed to fill this void.

Deep in my chest, anxiety knows how to *bite*.

And you say there's nothing special within its simplicity, and I ask, "How can you leave so willingly?"

You are missing the best part, and I should have known from the start,
not everyone deserves your heart.

I know what it feels like to want someone to carve out time for you, how you would run through the pouring rain to hand them your knife. Hoping then they'd create space for your presence.

But it took me so long to realize it is not my job to prove worthy. The ocean does not say, "Look at my beautiful waves; admire how I glow in the sun."

The ocean just is.

It can feel safer to tuck the petals of your heart into your pocket. After all, petals are fragile, and lately, the weather has been anything but forgiving.

Why would you want to expose your petals to such harsh conditions?

And even if the sun is peaking through the clouds, you can't be sure the conditions won't change.

So you keep the petals of your heart in your coat pocket, *claiming them as safe.*

But the other day, I saw petals dancing in the rain. I never realized one could dance happily in the pouring rain.

I thought we needed to guard the petals of our soul from ever feeling such misery. But these petals had been let go, and they looked… free.

I approached them and asked how they could still be so happy. "Look at this weather; the sun is nowhere," I explained to them.

They told me:

Sometimes it will rain and rain, but the sun is still there, even when you can't see it. It's the same with love…

Love doesn't exist anyless because a few of your heart petals are drenched in the rain of heartbreak.

Love is always there because you are nothing but pure, unconditional love.

We do not dance in the rain puddles because we like to feel the pangs of love.

We dance in the rain because we are love.

Deep conversations with friends or loved ones.

Trickling raindrops on my bedroom window.

The way my spine *shivers* when I submerge myself in a hot bath.

Twinkling lights on a summer night.

The first snow.

The way we bloom with the spring flowers after a long winter.

Feeling seen.

A deep belly laugh.

A helping hand.

Love.

Oblivion.

The inevitable truth is that no one will remember even the greatest of the greats one day.

* * *

And how we get to be here.

In this chaotic, tragic, and beautiful place we call our temporary ***home***.

The ocean must get so lonely. We ride the waves on the surface and admire the sea life coming up for air. We take in the vastness of its most visible layer, but we never absorb its *depth*.

The darkness of the ocean floor, the parts we dare not touch.

Our souls long for someone to reach inside our shells. Admiring the deepest parts of our most intricate selves.

The darkness that gives way to light.

All the pieces that make us…us.

I'm sitting on this old, worn-down bench, watching the sky dance between shades of tangerine, pastel, and aquamarine. Thinking to myself how love sometimes feels like a setting sun.

How we are all setting suns dancing by each other.

How am I to accept casual love when there is an elderly couple to my left? Cuddled up on their soft picnic blanket at the park. Two empty wine glasses lying in the grass beside them.

How am I to wish for anything other than everything when there is a young couple to my right? Arms intertwined, dancing to an old song.

We say such love no longer exists, but I found it at the local park today.
One to my left.. the other to my right.

I thought it would make me sad to be in the middle of such beautiful expressions of love. But instead, it only made me smile.

It was as if I had been led to the perfect spot. Like the universe was somehow aware I needed to remember such love still exists.

How it's happening around us, all the time.

We sometimes forget, intertwined within our own lives.

It can be easy to forget to look outside of ourselves.

I'm quite thankful the universe nudged me to look *to my left and right.*

I am not equipped for half-love.

It's like claiming the sunset as yours when you weren't there to see it shine.

Would you stay?

When time is no longer on my side, my hair begins to fade into a snowstorm of colors,
and we must slow down despite time speeding by us.

I want to know if your love can transcend beyond my physical body to a much deeper place. I want to know if your love wishes to make a home *beside* each other or if you wish only to create your own.

I want to know if your love can stretch through generations and never become too thin. Because you always made sure to nourish your soul first before loving mine.

I want to know if love means something more to you than a fleeting moment. If you see it as something as infinite as the stars above us.

But most of all,
I want to know if you will stay.

I don't want to be saved, altered, or re-invented through love. I want love to find me on a warm spring day, a glimmer of light shining on my cheekbones.

A feeling of radiance and longing and home *all at once.*

It's difficult to share the fragments of yourself that are not shiny and polished. For fear of someone seeing you as 'not enough.'

But the sun still shines on the cloudiest of days.

Without clouds, there would be no rain to nurture the Earth.

The clouds are necessary.

When someone asks how you are and says, "No, but really… how are you?".

Sitting silently with someone and not having to fill the space with empty words.

When someone says, "Hey, this made me think of you."

Going to a movie you would have never seen on your own time. But this human in your life loves it, and you love how *they light up when they talk about it.*

Being able to share your most vulnerable parts because every inch of your soul knows they see you.

For *exactly* all you are.

The type of person who supports your dreams, even when they are starting to come to life. Sometimes, even before you believe in them yourself.

Someone who will celebrate with you but also someone who will cry with you when the world becomes all too heavy.

The type of person who sees you as pure sunshine even when it rains.

A person whose *actions* say, "I see you, I hear you, I got you."

He saw me gazing up at the stars and asked which was my favorite, so I pointed to the bundle of stars shaped into the little dipper.

He said he would give them all to me, but I told him sometimes we must admire things from afar. No matter how much we wish, they were ours.

Even love wishes to be both held and free.

I wrote the ending of our story within the pages of my mind before the book even had a chance to come to life.

We all do this sometimes, trying to know the outcome ahead of time to shield our hearts.

But I remembered telling someone how beautiful it is to remain open. And how one day I hoped they would let someone into their heart.

I realized I had chewed my words and spit them out onto the concrete, unable to swallow my truth.

So now I'm not sure how to tell you I also feel terrified to keep my heart open.

Sometimes, love feels like someone putting a blindfold over my eyes and telling me to put something in my mouth.

How you never know if it will taste sweet or bitter. We may *need* the bitter to appreciate the sweet.

We may need to remind each other to swallow even the most bitter of loves. So that one day, when we taste a love so sweet and pure, we won't think twice before eating it whole.

Lately, I've been thinking about slow mornings and how I want to messily flip pancakes in the kitchen —my bare feet against the cool tile.

The aromas of freshly brewed coffee and the fresh flowers I grabbed from the farmers market the day before.

Floral and nutty and Earth all becoming one.

My phone left on my unmade bed, giving my mind a break from sensory overload, letting the sun shine through the windows, and allowing myself to immerse in the only moment of calm for my entire day.

I know there will always be more tasks, but there will only be this exact morning once.

I am feeling thankful for being here right *now*.

And it got me thinking about how lovely spending a slow morning with you would be.

I don't know who *'you'* are yet.

But sometimes, I can feel you in my bones.

And well, you would like the way I messily flip pancakes in my kitchen. The way I pour a cup of coffee in my oversized t-shirt, my bare feet dancing on the cool tile.

Letting ourselves immerse in each other, knowing it's not just another Monday. Because there won't ever be another moment like the one we get to be in right now.

The sun in me pouring warmth into the sun in you.

What if I told you the world knows no more than your soul?

There is this well I've been looking into, and at the bottom, I can see my reflection.

The pebble in my hand is a lot like the world around me. As soon as it slips through my fingers, it falls into the pits of my well and plops into the water —leaving my reflection distorted.

I can still see myself, but the edges around my cheekbones are no longer quite as soft. And everything is a bit blurry.

I'm trying to get the puddle to become still again so I can see myself. And not through the world's looking glass. But sometimes, it feels like pebbles are dropping from the sky, far outside my control, like many things.

It's not always about being a still, crisp puddle of your reflection.

Nothing is ever perfectly still.

The world is fast, chaotic, and ever-changing. And we're all trying to hang on and claim a little slice of happiness.

It's about choosing to see yourself for all that you are.

Even when things feel a little distorted, messy, and out of place.

Choosing to see yourself as whole anyway.

This feeling is inside my chest, and she keeps returning despite my disdain. Do you know her?

Her name is Ache.

She feels like longing, perching herself on my heart and breathing her presence into the space above my breasts.

She feels like a nuisance because she demands to be felt here and now.

But she is both the tension and the relief.

Because when I feel her for all she is, it's like standing in the pouring rain after your heart has been walking through the desert.

She shows me the pain but opens the door to my heart's desires. Telling me, "Stay a little longer, and you will see me as a beginning, not an end."

So I've been trying to sit with her, and I must say, the rain has never felt so good on my skin.

I used to try to fit into spaces too small for me.

Twisting. Bending. Folding.

All in the hopes I would fit—a missing puzzle piece discovered where everyone would cheer and applaud.

But shrinking myself only led to broken vessels and jagged puzzle edges.

Because you cannot force something that was never meant to fit in the first place, and I was never meant to be a piece of someone else's puzzle.

It took losing myself to the world's expectations to realize I contained all my puzzle pieces.

I haven't put all the pieces together yet; maybe we never do.

We are all continuing works of progress.

A masterpiece in the works is still a masterpiece, no?

I know our minds can play tricks on us. Making us feel we should shield our vulnerable feelings behind an old bookshelf—tucked away in the small attic space within our hearts.

I used to string my feelings together with a single bow and lock them there. Assuming they belonged somewhere unseen by the outside world.

But I started to miss the way vulnerability felt on my skin.

If you were to shrink yourself and climb into the attic space within my heart, you would find a single string lying on the floor. Because I finally let myself be all me again.

I let go of the feelings I thought I had to hide, the ones that were 'too much.'

Sometimes, we forget other people have their own locked attic spaces within their hearts. And sometimes, this means they do not have the capacity to experience all of you right now.

Perhaps, ever.

But this will never mean you should dim your light for fear of shining too bright.

It's always so unsettling; *falling*.

Climbing back on top of the tightrope after falling off is never a pretty sight. We don't copy and paste these moments into an aesthetically pleasing highlight reel. Instead, we only show the 0.25 seconds where we are quote-on-quote, "Living our best life."

But I wouldn't be standing here if I had never gotten back up—if I had refused to ugly crawl off the bathroom floor or out of my tiny studio bathtub.

The ground I have fallen unto is the Earth herself; she has always caught me, even when I could not do it on my own.

For I have always belonged to something much bigger than myself.

The rising lies in the falling.

I know I'm not ever *entirely* alone, but anxiety delights in telling me differently.

And today, I feel everything so deep, even the ocean herself wouldn't know what to do with this soul of mine.

So, I will give myself grace and breathe.

Letting myself be here, knowing soon enough, this storm will disappear.

Of what little can I give when all life is simply a setting sun and a breathing tide.

Two becoming one.

I'm reflective of my surroundings. But sometimes, I cannot tune into my own introverted ways when it becomes too much.

When I turn inwards to the point where I cannot see the door back out into the world.

I need to dive deep inside of myself, sometimes for days.

It's like stepping into a crisp, alpine lake and feeling born all over again.

But it's a balance, and I know I falter. I sometimes lean towards one side too harshly, sometimes not as much as I should.

How am I supposed to tell someone that when I look out at the sea, I don't just see an endless body of water... I see how the ocean and I aren't all that different...

Many people admire the surface of its waves but rarely dive into the depths of its being.

How do I explain to someone that the sunset feels like a sort of home I have never experienced? Or when I look up at the stars, it's not because they are sparkly and shiny. Instead, it makes me think about how small we are and how something can still shine in absolute darkness.

Even if it's a flicker.

Anxiety and I have lived together for many moons. I can never entirely rid myself of her, even when the sky of my mind is full of nothing but sunshine. And lately, she has been lingering closer to me, even though I told her I don't enjoy her presence.

But she asked me if she could buy me a cup of coffee and how could I turn down free coffee…

She told me to meet her at the local park. So I wandered through bustling sidewalks until I reached a quiet park with a single bench. And there she was, holding two cups of coffee. I thanked her for the cup of coffee and settled on the bench beside her.

A few moments went by without either of us saying anything.

It felt ironic Anxiety chose such a peaceful location. She has made me feel anything but peace over the years.

"I'm not sure what you want to talk about," I told her. "I don't know if we can be friends. I have tried many times, but it feels like we can never find a common ground, a peaceful ground".

Anxiety responded after a moment. "We need each other. I know I can be unbearable, crippling even. But you have taught me so much. I have learned how to breathe when the world is crumbling around me. I am learning to be at peace with unknown territories and difficult situations. That is all because of you."

"I think I have taught you a few things, too, even if they are more challenging lessons.", Anxiety said.

I didn't know what to say. I was shocked that she felt I had taught her things and even more surprised by how grateful she seemed. I had never thought she liked me very much.

"The truth is, you have taught me many things about myself," I responded. "You have shown me what it means to be human. You have taught me how to keep going even when I want to quit".

You placed me in front of a mirror and made me take a long, hard look at myself. And you made me choose.. me".

I continued, "You showed me I was much stronger than I thought I could be. And you pushed me in a way others cannot. But it still feels like a hard relationship, given our history".

Anxiety turned to me and said, "Sometimes we need our own space, and I know I have not always given that to you. But I can feel you pushing me away, and it only makes me want to cling to you more. And for that, I am sorry".

I placed my hand on top of hers. "Thank you. I understand so much better now. I, too, know what it is like to want to cling tight to someone out of fear of losing them. But we owe ourselves to let go because what is meant to stay will stay. Not only will they stay, but they will walk beside you, even in the pouring rain", I said.

We finished our coffee and sat in silence. After a while, it started to sprinkle, and then the sprinkle turned into a downpour. We covered our heads with our jackets and started walking out of the park. Both unable to hide the smiles within our hearts.

Anxiety and I, walking side by side in the pouring rain.

I don't mind alone time all that much. There are pieces of my soul that crave it and survive from such moments of solitude.

But recently, I've been craving something unfamiliar, a homecoming to a place I have yet to find.

How does such a feeling even exist?

I didn't know because it was one of those rare moments where I could not put it into logical words... *I could only feel it.*

I am trying to be here, but there is so much to do, and there will never be enough time to do everything this life has to give.

That may be why the knot in my throat swells when I think about picking what I want most out of this life.

It leaves me with this distasteful, raw feeling, like the way an oyster slides down the back of your throat. Smooth, but the taste is so strong it *lingers*.

The possibilities send shivers down my spine. I'm unsure if it's the fear of choosing wrong or the excitement of all the roads not yet taken.

All I know is there are curves along this road that match the curves of my body.

And all the searching I've been doing in these temporary spaces always led me *home*.

We call vulnerability frightening. But what scares me the most is denying myself the human experience of not being fully here. For the sake of being 'nonchalant'.

I've never known how to do such a thing,
how to take only dainty sips of intimacy and vulnerability.

I only know how to drink the whole glass.

I'm tired, but there's so much to see. I want to rest, but the sunset is calling my name. And this child is playing in the street, making me nostalgic for a time when life was much simpler.

But we make life more complicated as we grow.

Filling the passing time with mundane tasks we think will someday make us feel fulfilled. But we still feel even more disconnected from the Earth beneath our bare feet.

Tonight, I returned to my child-like roots, filling my bathtub with bubbles until it almost overflowed onto my navy blue fuzzy bathmat—my legs sticking out.

Even after all this time, I still want these simple moments.

I sometimes wonder if we make happiness this unattainable creature. An enigma of sorts. To the point where we have accepted it as a myth.

I don't mean the spurts of happiness we feel.

I mean the type of happiness that lasts.

The kind we don't get from the world but from within.

Because if so, we must shovel our way back to it every single day. Digging through the pollution of worldly strain—re-finding ourselves.

More importantly, *choosing* to find ourselves.

Again and again.

I want to ask Mother Nature if she can turn down the volume, but thunderstorms demand to exist even when we want nothing but sunshine.

Even when we are tired of the wind blowing us every way but never to a place that feels like home.

Mother Nature heard my pleas and felt no pity.

She said, *"My child, if I give you nothing but sunshine, you will cry out to be cleansed and made new again by my rain."*

You are still heard, even in the pouring rain, because the soul does not need to speak to be seen.

The soul just is.

If I could talk to Uncertainty herself, she would say, "Hello, I am all life's uncertainties. I am those times in life where you don't know what will be next. Welcome to my home; I've wanted to talk to you".

I'd perch myself on her chair, hoping she could finally explain what would happen next.

To my dismay, she would do none of these things.

Uncertainty said, "I cannot tell you what will happen next. I am the space before that moment. The one you humans find uncomfortable to the point of avoiding any change at all. I can only tell you these feelings of discomfort are signals that you are very close to growth. And that it won't always be at the most convenient time. For time has no consideration for your personal life".

All life is change. *And you can attempt to protect yourself from these growing pains. But you will miss out on what it means to live free among the wildflowers.*

Breathe grace into these unknown spaces and then let go.

Of the need to control or protect or know.

Be here. Learn here. Feel here. Observe here.

This is the time to take up space and not apologize finally.

Trying something new but doing it only for myself and no one else.

Learning how to be comfortable in the silence of my own company.

Buying myself flowers, cooking homemade pasta, or going on a road trip with friends.

This time is dedicated to me.

There is still something important to learn here, something I can't yet see.

Everything is connected.

All this unknown space is welcoming me.

To something more beautiful than I could ever have imagined.

We watch the sun fade into nothing
and call it beautiful.

We, too, fade as time passes
thinning skin and fragile bones,
yet we don't call it beautiful like the sunset.

But weren't those lines around your lips formed
from all the years you spent smiling and laughing
as you watched the sun fade
and called it beautiful.

I love the smell of the damp earth after it rains. I love how dew drips off succulent plants in the morning, how children jump in puddles, and how my coffee pot gurgles as it spurts out aromas of morning decadence. I love the frothy white foam each wave creates as it reaches the shore. And if you listen closely, a musical ripple erupts from the stones underneath. I love the feeling when you submerge your shoulders in a hot bath, sending shivers down your spine. *I love deep conversations that remind you of what this life is all about—how a hug can make you feel both held and free. How the sky turns into a work of art every single night, and it's free to watch. But mostly, I love how I get to be here for it. And even when this life feels agonizingly heavy, light can peak through the cracks, like* a weed creeping through the space between sidewalk steps.

How, despite the odds, it grows anyway.

These aching crevices are within my bones, and I cannot tell if they are yearning for rest or wishing to run free among the wildflowers.

Sometimes, it feels like I am being pulled in both directions.

To rest but be active. To give myself space. But not to the point where I can no longer appreciate the human ability to connect, share, and learn from others.

Growing pains never really go away.

Such aches travel to our hearts as we age and try to figure out where we belong in this world.

I will take you to the biggest concert venue and plug an aux cord into my chest.

And then you will understand why sometimes words cannot explain *this heart of mine.*

If I could become the entire ocean,
would I feel safe within the depths of her core

or would I cling to the waves
and call it *clarity*

It's true, you cannot read my mind.

But sometimes I wish you could because today my mind is a sandstorm. And I am a single spec of sand whirling about within it.

I know these moments pass, and I know I can handle them. But sometimes I wish with all my heart I didn't have to weather these storms alone.

I met Pain at the local café. I had been putting off our reunion for quite some time. I kept telling her I was busy. I wasn't. Unless you count distracting yourself with outside activities to avoid internal feelings, she knew this, though.

I grabbed my usual—an iced oat milk latte. And she got her regular—black coffee. I realized avoiding her inevitably meant I was avoiding the deepest parts of myself.

And didn't those pieces deserve to be felt, too?

But sometimes, it felt like too much for one human to carry.

She listened, as she always did, and responded, "I am inevitable in this world. But I was never meant to live in your heart. *If we were to hold onto all of the stars, how would we ever be able to see them shine?"*.

I sat there, listening as she continued, "You have to let me go. It doesn't mean you won't ever think of me or feel my presence. It just will allow you to make room in your heart for better things".

"Like love?" I asked.
"*Yes, especially love,"* she responded.

I've thought of time ceaselessly, even though I know it's an *unreciprocated* love.

Time cannot think.

Time has never thought once about me or you or anyone, yet we somehow find ways to blame time for so many things.

Frustrations, doubts, fears, heartbreak.

And if it's not enough time, it's too much time, and if it's too much time, it's not enough.

We may always want more days of this life when our hourglass runs dry. But we may feel ready, as ready as one can ever be.

Who is to know?

Many moons ago, I laid my worries in a field full of life.

I plucked a single dandelion from the ground
and raised it to my lips.

As I took a deep breath, I gathered all the
despair, fear, and worry tucked deep inside
my heart.

And when I breathed out, the dandelion stems flew
into the blue sky.

I imagined each stem holding onto something I had let go of,
out of me and into the world.

And instead of the world receiving all my emotions and worries,
each dandelion stem transformed into a butterfly.

Peaceful and free and born to fly.

Be here. Be here. Be here.

We hear this everywhere. We know we should, and yet when we are left to our own devices, it feels agonizing. Lately, my mind has been begging for space to breathe. To not fill it with more tasks or to-do lists.

It's asking me to do something so simple.

Be here.

My feet have grown tired from running around over things that will never matter. A peace of its own kind lies in the nape of my neck. Its pulse brings me back whenever the world starts to pull me away.

It smiles and says,

You are here

You are here.

You

are

Here.

There is a palm tree I can see from my back patio. She stands tall and sturdy, but her presence feels delicate.

Other palm trees are grouped to her right, but she has this orb of solitude around her entire being. Sometimes, I wish I could ask if she ever feels lonely, having so much space.

Late at night, I can almost imagine what she would say to a soul like me.

It would go something like this:

"Space has given me a different type of embrace. It can be easy only to see how my branches and leaves are not intertwined with those around me. But I don't mind. *I like how the sun can touch all of me, even how* I can feel every drop of rain when it storms. I know you can't see them from where you are standing. But my roots connect to all the other living things extending far and wide, so I am never alone."

I hope you remember that you are also rooted in this earth, connected to every living being.

An impromptu decision led me to a forest filled with pine trees, good company, and the pouring rain. We usually grumble under our breath about the rain, how it never rains according to our schedule.

How amused the rain must be, watching us all fuss over the Earth herself.. over things we cannot control.

I couldn't remember the last time I stood outside in the pouring rain—surrounded by pine trees and good company. And in that moment, I couldn't think of anywhere else I'd rather be.

I had missed the smell of fresh rain against the Earth.

Do you know the one I am referring to?

It might sound cliche, but it felt like I was being cleansed from all the invisible weight I had piled onto my chest.

From all the things I felt I needed to control.

But the rain reminded me how much I cannot control and how beautiful it can feel if we accept it for what it is—if we let it nourish us as much as it cleanses the Earth.

We also need the rain to let go.

So, we, too, can grow.

If I were a tree, would I become tired of standing in one spot for my entire life
or would my roots stretch far and wide, helping me stay strong?

We admire the tree but scarcely respect the roots. They're not pleasing to look at; most of the time, they hide beneath the Earth.

But the roots are the foundation, and without them, there would be
no tree to admire,
no spring flowers to watch bloom,
no autumn leaves to watch fall.

I'm trying not to overthink the future, but everyone around me is planning for their whole life —and I'm trying to make friends with this mind of mine.

I've learned thoughts are only thoughts, and I am the one who notices.

But it's taking every ounce of me not to fall into old thinking patterns—or plan spontaneous adventures to escape sitting with these feelings.

To observe how the birds know to start singing when the sun rises. How the ocean shore feels under my toes and all the beautiful mountains I've climbed.

A picture inside my mind and heart and nowhere within my phone.

How can we stay present when we always think about what the rest of our lives will be?

When I'm trying to love my family, be fully present in my relationships, read books, keep my heart open, and fall in love.

If you are reading this, *who* is the one reading?

Is it the one who observes how spring flower petals fall to the ground at the end of spring? Or is it the one who feels nostalgic as the seasons change?

Is the one who experienced what it was like to jump in a puddle not still the same you who avoids stepping in them today?

Because if the ocean was once something you feared before you learned to swim, isn't it still the same ocean you have grown to love today?

Some nights, these rocks perch on my chest, and feel anything but human. Maybe it's because we are accustomed to highlight reels and sparkling interiors.

Even though all things rust over time.

But isn't that beautiful too?

Something can be here for so long despite the world changing around it. It has seen and weathered many storms, and yet, it remains.

We, too, rust with time.

We are missing the point of beauty, the rustic, undeniable human beauty that comes from the cycle of life. No matter how many new things we make, they will become aged and worn down.

We quickly greet the glitter and throw away the cobwebs collected on old, rustic books.

But what about our old souls as time passes?

What about old loves, old memories, and the ever-passing time?

Can we be kinder to those parts of ourselves?
Letting the sun splash glitter on the rustic pieces of ourselves that have aged with time.

Can we still see it as beautiful?

The thing is, we don't have all the time in the world.

We hear stories of people who run out of time too quickly, but we never think it will happen to us—not truly, anyway.

As if we are somehow less mortal.

While every living, breathing organism around us is *here one moment and gone the next.*

The wilted sunflowers on your kitchen table, the lilac flowers that have fallen to the earth at the end of spring, a monarch butterfly taking its final bow.

And while we see this life cycle, we don't grasp it—
clinging to its truth with tethered heartstrings.

How something can be both momentary and lasting within our hearts.

How we are physically impermanent, but our souls remain.

If I were to watch myself in this time of solitude and self-reflection, would I form a greater sense of self-love?

My private, mundane moments—like a fly on the wall.

Would I finally see how beautiful it all is?

How it's all connected.

Would I find a new sense of strength after watching how I tremble in the darkness? Tears streaming down my face while driving down the highway— to then see myself take a deep breath, wipe the tears, and continue to move forward.

Would I admire my long legs, seeing how far they take me every moment of every single day? To the summits and valleys and everywhere in between. Would I laugh at the way I dance to music when I am all alone? Bare feet against the wooden floor, hairbrush propped up as a microphone.

I've been trying to observe myself more.

To be here, wherever that is.

Finally, I claim myself as loved…by *me*.

When the pangs of boredom enter the proximity of my mind, something inside of me tenses—wanting to shove it away. To distract myself with something, anything.

There is something unfamiliar and unsettling with boredom in the 21st century. We often find it distasteful and want to do everything we can to prevent it from becoming an option.

I remember complaining to my mother as a child about how bored I was, and she would tell me, "Good, it means you have time to imagine… time to create…time to think". I didn't quite understand what she meant until much later in life.

I realize she was saying something so simple—yet so profound.

She was asking a question without asking it at all…

How can we create, dream, or imagine if we are always in a constant state of busyness?

One of the synonyms for boredom is discontent. It makes me wonder if we have placed boredom and unhappiness in the same category. Or if it's because sometimes we need to understand what it feels like to be discontent. So we can learn where the uncomfortable grooves in our personal lives need *more care...*

more grace...

more observance...

I had my morning coffee with an old friend.

Her name is Solitude.

Sometimes, I avoid her with every ounce of my being—and other times, I don't know how to let go of her. Our relationship can be tricky; like most things, it ebbs and flows. She is the type of friend you can go without seeing for a while. Knowing you'll always be there for each other no matter how much time passes.

Solitude sipped her lavender latte as she spoke, "Many people confuse me with loneliness. But we couldn't be more different. One can feel lonely with too much of me, but I create space for breathing. I sometimes feel I am the closest thing to slowing down time".

I thought about this on my walk home, her words replaying in my head like your favorite album on repeat.

We tend to confuse being alone with being lonely.

What if we welcomed solitude?

Would we all know ourselves a little better? Would we be more present in our daily lives? Would we feel more connected to our deepest selves?

Will we miss these moments of solitude when they no longer come so free?

Will we have wished to enjoy such moments more?

Rather than agonize over the day we no longer have to endure endless nights with only our own company.

Can we pour gratitude into the silence?

We have the tendency to close,
a sparse attempt to protect ourselves.

But what if we let go? What if we breathe light into these unknown spaces?

What if the light you have been seeking was always you?

Triggers in our hearts can be a lot like the trigger of a gun. Because you don't always realize you have them until it's already been fired.

It hits you all at once, and then you find yourself saying, "Oh, this affects me in a way I didn't expect."

It's easy to want to mute such triggers or call them melodramatic for fear of being too much. But they are honest and thus valid.

We can analyze how something affects us and be mindful of the way we respond to the catalyst for that trigger.

We can still set boundaries to create space for our healing.

We can notice how other people do not usually intend to ignite such flames. And still, allow ourselves the grace of being human.

I think it's the only way we can ever work towards releasing our triggers—or at least *softening their edges*.

We owe ourselves to listen to such moments and remain open.

Isn't it odd—how we know we are beneath the blue sky but hardly ever take a moment to admire the wispy cloud formations or;

Steam rising from your favorite coffee mug, flower petals on sidewalk streets—telling us summer is near, a dandelion blowing in the wind, the crease left behind a smile, golden hour shadows dancing whimsically across your bedroom wall, vines wrapping themselves around rusted gates.

I want to say thank you to each of them for showing me beauty in small, intimate moments.

For reminding me, the sky is no less beautiful just because the clouds feel a little heavier some days.

Isn't it beautiful?

How life continues to move us
towards where we are meant to be.

There is a single flower standing proudly on the cracked sidewalk. How quickly it will be plucked away, seen as a mere mistake.

I wanted to protect it, but removing it from its home would mean ripping it from the roots which have given it life.

So I left it there, admiring how it grew despite the cement telling it not to. It made me think of all the places we go.

How sometimes we must grow in uncomfortable places, sometimes on our own.

And despite our growing pains, our roots spread wide wherever we wander.

Until — we, too — bloom within spaces once deemed too difficult.

Crazy,
how easy it is to fill
our lives with the most
insignificant of things.

Nobody likes to let themselves feel distasteful emotions. And when we see someone feeling their emotions in public, we become uncomfortable.

What is it about humans and the need to appear so put together all the time?

I don't even think we know.

We just follow suit.

And so we hold it all inside until we are in the privacy of our cars or curled up on the bathroom floor, and then we … release it.

We are meant to release.

Again and again and again.

The cycle of becoming undone to be put back together and made new.

We admire how long a tree can stand
but I often wonder if they ever
wish to lie down.

If they, too become tired,
after withstanding
many storms.

After a few steps onto the wooden bridge, I can feel the uneasiness of the boards beneath my feet.

The wind continues to blow despite how bad I wish it would be still, for even a *moment*.

Doesn't it know I'm trying to get to the other side?

Doesn't it know my knees are already shaky?

These bones worn

d
  o
    w
      n

But the birds sing, oblivious to the wind or unbothered by its presence—happy to be here while the wind dances through their feathers.

The birds have known they would never be able to change the wind. No matter how much they would prefer stillness instead.

It got me thinking that we, too, can learn to sing— despite the winds of life.

My mountain said, "You have to feel the lows so you can fully experience the highs."

She was right; the lows felt unbearable, but the highs felt so beautiful. I wouldn't have tasted the highs as delicious if I hadn't experienced the bitter taste of the lows.

It can be hard to remind yourself of these things when you feel stuck in the valleys—when you can't yet see how beautiful the view will be because it feels like you have been climbing the same mountain for eternity.

And when you thought you reached the top, it was only the halfway point, a resting point. One that you very much needed, yet now you feel afraid to continue the journey.

Because you still have no idea what the top of the mountain will look like. What if it's not everything you had hoped for? What if it's worse?

And how can we find peace during these periods of stagnation and unknowing?

As if reading my thoughts, the Mountain responded:

"Remember what I said about highs and lows, how you need the valleys to appreciate the mountain tops. But there is one thing I forgot to mention. *You see, you also need the spaces between.* The moments when you are traveling to your destination and feel stuck along the way. Tired and worn down and defeated. These moments matter the most", said the Mountain.

"Well, this part doesn't feel good at all. How could this be helpful to me?" I ask.

My mountain said, "My dear, it is all connected. *You have been living inside your head too much. Trying to control the outcome when my mountain top will be what it is, regardless of how much you worry.* Can't you see you are well on your way now? The sunrise will never look the same from where you are standing. There is beauty here, too; you must remember to look for it".

So up I went, noticing how the sunrise **danced** along my mountain. How it hadn't looked that way before, and how it would continue to change as I kept moving forward.

How do you let go of something that was never yours? / What am I meant to do in this life? / Are we ever supposed to know? / Is there only one 'right' answer?

If the universe is listening, I am asking for a sign.

I am here.

Listening.

Waiting.

I am trying to remember the fragility of all things.

For we are here and then gone
and I ache to remain present for the moments between.

I'm strolling through an ocean town, admiring the shops and strangers around me and wondering if they can tell how tired my bones are—if any of them feel the same. If they would rather be at home, snuggled up in bed.

Even more so, if they wish they had someone to tuck them in and plant a kiss on their forehead.

And who is to know what will come
of the love we give
or the love we take.

Who is to know,
for I do not know.

I often wonder how many loves we throw away.

The eye contact we avoided in the grocery store.

The phone call we didn't make.

The idea we need to have our entire lives figured out before letting ourselves be vulnerable.

As if we could have ever known the ending.

What would happen if we said hello to more strangers?

If we made the phone call.

If we kept our hearts open *despite* the unknown.

Would we find something else to worry over if we did know?

Is this the human condition? Always seeking answers we weren't meant to uncover.

Always half satisfied with where we are at. Because letting ourselves be fully satisfied feels like some weakness—breaking our hearts all for the sake of some predetermined idea of what happiness means.

Can we find peace in releasing our souls of the job to know what lies ahead?

Can we pour gratitude into what is right now?

The truth is, I don't know what's next, and it feels terrifying.

How do we balance letting the universe guide us while still being proactive in our dreams?

If all the universe is a haystack and my hand is my dream, how do I know how to find the needle without poking my finger along the way?

I used to worry about choosing wrong. Sometimes, it feels like I have no choice but to get it right the first time. Because there is so much to do, and time seems to speed up as each year passes.

But I'm learning it's less about choosing 'right' and more about leaning into the things that nourish your soul.

I'm trying to appreciate how the sun reflects on the evening water. The way a hug feels when you need it more than knowing what the future holds and how gazing up at the stars makes you feel so small yet so alive.

These moments bring me a sense of peace more remarkable than any concrete evidence of my future.

Does such evidence even exist?

Because nothing about where this life will lead me feels definite.

The universe has a way of bending my concrete plans with its pliers until they become something new.

The ocean and the sun are the closest we can ever get to a state of knowing.

They exist.

May we spend less time trying to know the answers and more time letting the evening tide take us to places of love.

I've laid a towel down on a speckled blanket of sand. Many of those specs have escaped their home and found their way between my toes and against my thighs. The sun radiates its warmth, bringing life back to my sleepy eyes.

Children are playing in the water, unaware of how cold it is, or perhaps they know something we forget as we grow older.

We call children silly dreamers and wishful thinkers. But what dream birthed itself from the womb of anything realistic or orderly?

Weren't we once dreamers, too?

I cling to small moments because we are a collection of moments strung together by an invisible string.

I am trying not to take the gift of observation for granted. Like a child who has picked flowers, unaware they are weeds.

How the child still sees them as beautiful.

There are parts of me exhausted by the weight of trying to fit my broken pieces back together. But some pieces are no longer symmetrical and have worn-down edges—their colors faded by the moon and sun cycle.

Can we even put such pieces back together again?

Is it okay if some of them no longer fit? Everything changes constantly, and I have outgrown many pieces of my past self.

They aren't less important or any less of me; they just no longer fit quite like they used to. I have spent so much time trying to glue old pieces of myself back together, afraid I will become lost again if I don't.

But like the shoes I have outgrown, I can not squeeze my entire soul into fragments of my past self.

It makes no sense to walk around in shoes two sizes too small, so why do we try to squeeze into spaces we have outgrown?

It's frightening to let go. We worry about trying to keep the puzzle pieces of ourselves together that we forget our souls will always be intact.

Sometimes, the pieces of our experiences, memories, and emotions will feel out of control—making us feel messy and broken.

But the soul remains put together because it was never torn apart to begin with.

All these pieces we had outgrown were leading us back home all along. Our experiences may not always make sense as a whole.

But that's okay.

We would never find our way back to our true selves if everything always fit perfectly.

If dreams are passageways to the soul, then maybe they're trying to tell me something by their recurring nature. All I remember when I wake up are the various doors I walked through and the winding roads driven.

Always going somewhere, but it never feels quite like home.

And recently, my soul has been aching to find my sanctuary. But all the doors and roads have only led me to temporary ones.

Always going somewhere, but not quite feeling at home.

It is a different kind of ache- when home isn't what you thought it would be, yet you feel so close.

And while I will always be my own home, *there is a longing for these roots of mine to sink their teeth into the ground.*

And call it homely.

If I had to choose to be the wave or the entire ocean — I would choose the ocean.

Because while you admire the waves, I admire the depth.

They tell us not to compare, but has this world not made it seem like we must constantly compete to be the best?

We can only compete with ourselves, but confusing the 'self' with the world is easy.

Realizing you were competing for something outside of yourself.

It's all so confusing, and I think we make it this way as humans.

We like to overthink and over-analyze and call it normal.

"Silver Lining!" I cry out, "Are you there?".

I've been searching for weeks, and she is nowhere. I look out onto the horizon, but it feels like I'm missing the sunset by a fraction of a second—silver replaced by dark, starry nights.

"Silver Lining, don't you know I need you?" I protest.

It feels like she has become a figment of my imagination or something I was told as a child while tucked into bed, a fairytale.

"Silver Lining, I promise never to take you for granted again," I say.

Even a glimpse of her would feel like a saving grace for this weary heart. I don't know what's next, which isn't very comforting.

I also made a few mistakes along the way, and I'm trying to see the purpose of the teardrops that have fallen onto my tank top. But seeing how this could turn into something beautiful feels so hard.

"I am here," Silver Lining says.

"I have always been here. I do not live within the stars or among the most beautiful sunsets. I am the silver string wrapped around your entire soul—an infinite line with neither a beginning nor an end. Sometimes, you cannot feel me because pain and sadness and anger and fear can feel much bigger. You must feel these things before you can feel all of me", she says.

"Silver Lining, I've missed you," I say.

She said, "My dear, can't you see that I am as much a part of you as you are to me. Can't you see how we are intertwined infinitely. Do you see it now? How you are the silver lining?".

It has always been you.

I sometimes imagine there is a lock around my soul.

Alpine lakes and mountain peaks to keep out intruders, a guard standing idle outside my door.

Sometimes, keys can be deceiving—twisting and wriggling their way through until it fits.

Naturally, when this happens, you believe whoever has entered must be the one you've been waiting for. Only after time has passed do you realize the key doesn't fit that well inside your heart.

How it aches in places where the edges are slightly more jagged.

I've grown tired of the lessons provided through such keys. And lately, I have wished for the key to fit more than anything.

But I am learning all keys have their purpose.

To remind me what I want, what I deserve, what I am worthy of.

And what a funny thought—that in today's world, we must make room
for our thoughts.

They're here, I know it.

I can feel them trying to push through the brick door in the back of my head—pushing against the weight of expectational intruders. Each one of them fighting to stay in the front.

While my thoughts and ideas collect dust on the bookshelf behind the brick door.

But my ideas, thoughts, and dreams are…

Valid.

Worthy.

They can live on some old, abandoned bookshelf in your local library when it is time for me to move on from this temporary home to wherever we go next.

But for now, they deserve to feel the warmth of the sun.

They deserve to live.

I have no desire to be the entire ocean.

I am but a single drop of salt water.

There are billions of other drops; still, only one is you. It's easy to start to feel like we are the entire ocean when we are collectively one gigantic body of water.

It's easy to forget the other drops of water are not you.

They may be a part of you, but you cannot claim something vast and beyond yourself.

I sat beneath the weeping willow, the branches draping over me like a warm blanket.

The old tree began to weep.

"Why do you weep?" I asked.

The tree responded, "I have been standing here for so long. I have watched the sunset and moon rise for over 100 years. And during that time, countless souls have come to me for my warm embrace—a place to seek comfort and solitude after heartbreak or loss. A safe place to dream and contemplate the meaning of life. *It is almost as if I, too, experienced it —feeling the weight of it all as each soul leaned against me*".

I was quiet momentarily, taking in every word. Finally, I said, "There is a certain loneliness in being able to feel everything so deeply."

I placed my hand on the tree trunk—each ripple representing the tree's long life.

"Far too many souls will never understand the beautiful curse planted within you. If you could choose to feel nothing, would you?" I asked.

The weeping willow responded, "No, to feel nothing would be death itself. A mere whisper into the void, a wasted spec of sand in the universe. I would rather experience the suffering that comes with feeling it all. In doing so, I honor the universe for all she is, all she was, and all she is yet to be".

We are all a part of the universe, the only truth I know.